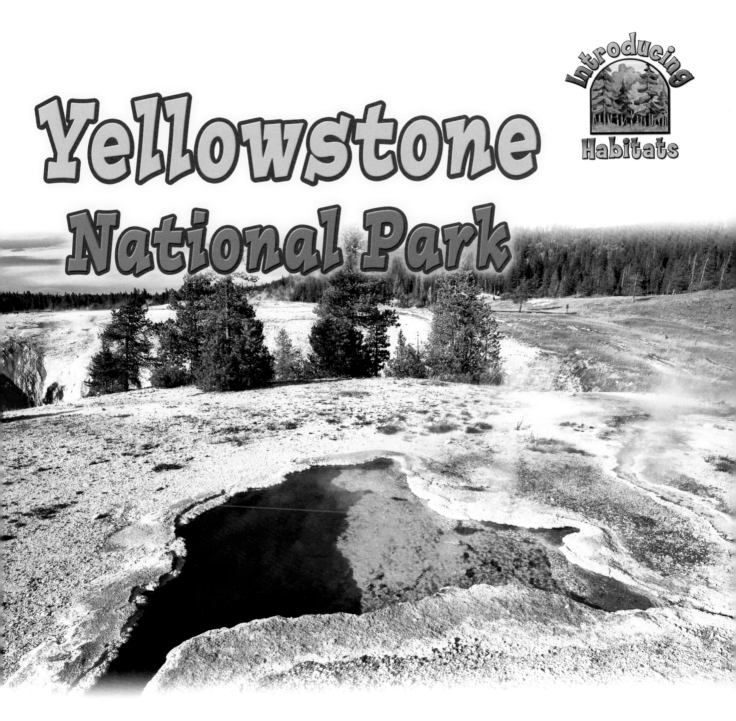

Yellowstone National Park

Bobbie Kalman

🍄 Crabtree Publishing Company

www.crabtreebooks.com

Introducing Habitats

Created by Bobbie Kalman

With gratitude, for my wonderful friend Enlynne Paterson,
who supports and inspires me

Author and Editor-in-Chief
Bobbie Kalman

Research
Enlynne Paterson

Editor
Kathy Middleton

Proofreader
Crystal Sikkens

Photo research
Bobbie Kalman

Design
Bobbie Kalman
Katherine Berti
Samantha Crabtree (cover)

Production coordinator
Katherine Berti

Illustrations
Barbara Bedell: page 23 (coyote)
Vanessa Parson-Robbs: page 23 (beaver)

Photographs
BigStockPhoto: pages 11 (top), 24 (bottom)
Shutterstock: cover, pages 1, 3, 4, 5, 6–7, 8, 9,
    10, 11 (bottom), 12, 13 (left), 14, 15, 16 (top),
    17, 18, 19, 20, 21, 22, 23, 24 (top), 25 (bottom),
    26, 27, 28, 29, 30, 31 (top)
NPS Photo by Jim Peaco: page 31 (bottom)
Other images by Photodisc

Library and Archives Canada Cataloguing in Publication

Kalman, Bobbie, 1947-
    Yellowstone National Park / Bobbie Kalman.

(Introducing habitats)
Includes index.
ISBN 978-0-7787-2961-7 (bound).--ISBN 978-0-7787-2989-1 (pbk.)

    1. Habitat (Ecology)--Yellowstone National Park--Juvenile literature.
2. Natural history--Yellowstone National Park--Juvenile literature.
I. Title. II. Series: Introducing habitats

QH105.W8K34 2010   j577.09787'52   C2009-903779-3

Library of Congress Cataloging-in-Publication Data

Kalman, Bobbie.
    Yellowstone National Park / Bobbie Kalman.
        p. cm. -- (Introducing habitats)
    Includes index.
    ISBN 978-0-7787-2989-1 (pbk. : alk. paper) -- ISBN 978-0-7787-2961-7
(reinforced library binding : alk. paper)
    1. Natural history--Yellowstone National Park.--Juvenile literature. 2.
Habitat (Ecology)--Yellowstone National Park--Juvenile literature. I. Title.
II. Series.

QH105.W8K35 2010
508.787'52--dc22

                                                          2009024179

Crabtree Publishing Company
www.crabtreebooks.com   1-800-387-7650

Published in Canada
Crabtree Publishing
616 Welland Ave.
St. Catharines, ON
L2M 5V6

Published in the United States
Crabtree Publishing
PMB16A
350 Fifth Ave., Suite 3308
New York, NY 10118

Published in the United Kingdom
Crabtree Publishing
Maritime House
Basin Road North, Hove
BN41 1WR

Published in Australia
Crabtree Publishing
386 Mt. Alexander Rd.
Ascot Vale (Melbourne)
VIC 3032

Contents

The first national park

When explorers from the eastern United States first saw Yellowstone, they could not believe their eyes! The variety of animals and huge numbers of **geysers**, **hot springs**, and waterfalls filled them with wonder (see pages 28-31). The explorers felt that the area should be set aside for all people to enjoy. In 1872, the government agreed and made Yellowstone the world's first **national park**. A national park is an area of land that is protected by a government so plants and animals can live there safely. Other countries also set aside areas to become national parks, such as Banff National Park in Canada. It became a national park in 1885. Today, there are thousands of national parks in the world.

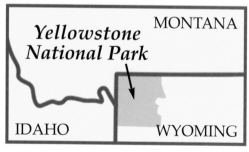

Yellowstone is located in the states of Wyoming, Montana, and Idaho, but most of the park is in Wyoming.

4

What is an ecosystem?

Yellowstone National Park is part of the Greater Yellowstone **Ecosystem**. In an ecosystem, everything is connected. **Living things** work together with other living things and with the **non-living** parts of their environment. Plants and animals are living things. Sunlight, air, rocks, soil, and water are non-living things.

sun

bear

water

rock

soil

deer

Yellowstone is home to animals such as bears, wolves, bison, deer, and elk. Name three living things you can see on this page. Name four non-living things.

plants

Yellowstone habitats

The Yellowstone Ecosystem has several kinds of **habitats**. Habitats are the natural homes of plants and animals. Some Yellowstone habitats are forests, mountains, and grasslands. There are also water habitats in Yellowstone, such as rivers, **streams**, and lakes. Streams are small rivers. Name all the habitats you see on these two pages.

mountain

forest

grassland

stream

7

Food chains in habitats

Plants and animals find everything they need in their habitats. First, they need **energy**. Energy is the power to grow, move, and stay alive. Energy comes from the sun. Plants use the sun's energy to turn air and water into food. Using sunlight to make food is called **photosynthesis**.

sun

Plants take in sunlight and air through their leaves. They get water through their roots. When a mule deer eats a plant's leaves, it is getting the sun's energy. How does it do that?

What is a food chain?

Plants use the sun's energy to make food, but animals cannot make their own food. They get energy by eating other living things. The sun's energy is passed along a **food chain**. The food chain on this page follows energy from the sun, to plant leaves, to a deer, and then to a wolf. Yellowstone habitats have many food chains.

Plants use the sun's energy to make food. The sun's energy is inside the plants.

Deer eat the leaves of trees and bushes. When they eat, the sun's energy is passed along to them.

When a wolf eats a deer, the sun's energy is passed from the plants the deer eats, to the deer, and then to the wolf. The wolf now has the sun's energy in its body.

*Deer are **herbivores**. Herbivores are animals that eat mainly plants.*

*Wolves are **carnivores**. Carnivores are animals that eat other animals. Wolves are also **predators**. Predators hunt the animals they eat.*

9

Pine forests

Forests are habitats with mainly trees and some other plants. Forests of **conifers** grow throughout Yellowstone National Park. Conifers are trees with cones and needle-like leaves. Most of the conifers in Yellowstone are lodgepole pine trees. Many animals find food and shelter in these pine-forest habitats.

lodgepole pine tree

Elk, or wapiti, live in the forests of Yellowstone. Elk are large deer. They are herbivores that eat leaves, flowers, grasses, and other plants.

(above) Wolves are carnivores that hunt elk, deer, and other forest animals. These wolves are eating a deer they have hunted. (left and below) Bald eagles make nests high on the pine trees of Yellowstone. Eagles are birds called **raptors**. Raptors catch animals with the **talons**, or claws, on their feet.

talons

11

Mountain habitats

mountain lion

There are mountains all around Yellowstone.
Mountains are the habitats of many living things.
Few plants grow at the top of mountains because it is
too cold and windy, but trees and other plants grow
at the bottom of mountains. Bears, wolves, pikas,
bighorn sheep, and mountain lions look for food in
the mountains of Yellowstone. This mountain lion is
looking for animals to eat in its mountain habitat.

12

Mountain climbers

Animals such as mountain goats and bighorn sheep, shown right, are **adapted**, or suited, to living in mountain habitats. They can walk and climb on rocks because they have **hooves**. Hooves are tough coverings that protect the feet of these animals.

bighorn sheep

pika

Tiny pikas

Pikas are cousins of rabbits. They have short legs and tails and rounded ears. Most pikas live on rocky mountainsides. They live in the holes between the rocks. Pikas are herbivores that feed on grasses, twigs, and leaves. Coyotes, eagles, bears, and mountain lions eat pikas.

What are grasslands?

Grasslands are flat areas of land that are covered with grasses. Bushes and flowers also grow on grasslands, but there are not many trees. Grasslands cover some areas of Yellowstone National Park. **Meadows** are grasslands that grow beside streams and rivers. Herbivores such as bison find plenty of food to eat in Yellowstone's meadows.

Gizzly bears are **omnivores**. Omnivores eat both plants and animals. Grizzlies look for food in most of Yellowstone's habitats. They eat pine bark and pine nuts in the forests, small animals in the mountains, and fish they catch in the rivers and lakes. During early spring, grizzlies hunt baby elk and bison on the grasslands. They also eat the grasses and flowers that grow in meadows, such as this one.

Water habitats

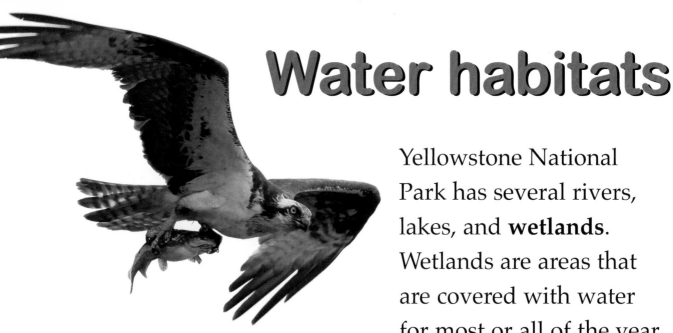

Osprey are raptors. They love to eat fish. This osprey has caught a fish with its talons and is carrying its meal home.

Yellowstone National Park has several rivers, lakes, and **wetlands**. Wetlands are areas that are covered with water for most or all of the year. All these habitats contain **fresh water**. Fresh water does not have a lot of salt. Plants grow in the water, and fish and birds live in or on it. Other animals come to drink and bathe in these water habitats.

These raccoons have come to a river to drink water. They also eat any fish, frogs, or other animals they find. Raccoons are omnivores.

The trumpeter swan is the biggest North American bird. Trumpeter swans feed on plants that grow in the shallow waters of rivers and lakes.

These swan **cygnets**, or baby swans, are looking for food. One is dipping its head under water to eat some plants.

A moose is also finding plants to eat in the shallow waters of a wetland. Moose are the biggest deer. They are larger than elks.

Four seasons

Yellowstone National Park has four seasons. They are autumn, winter, spring, and summer. Each season has different weather. In autumn, the grasses and some trees turn golden yellow and then brown. The nights are colder, and it rains or snows.

In autumn, male elks make bugling sounds to bring female elks into the area for **mating**.

In spring, wildflowers bloom, and baby animals are born. This baby black bear is tasting some spring grasses and flowers.

In winter, the weather is freezing cold, and it snows. Bison search for plants buried under the snow.

In summer, the weather is hot. People come to Yellowstone to see the amazing sights (see pages 28-31). They also come to fish, hike, swim, and go canoeing. This child is dipping his feet into a cool lake.

19

Story of the bison

The American bison is the largest land animal in North America. About 130 years ago, there were millions of bison. Ten years later, there were fewer than 1,000! People hunted almost all the bison, but Yellowstone National Park helped some bison stay alive. The park gave them a safe place to live. Today, there are about 3,500 bison in Yellowstone.

*Bison babies are called **calves**. Calves are born in the spring. They can stand soon after they are born.*

A bison mother gives birth to one calf at a time. The calf drinks its mother's milk for about seven months.

As well as drinking milk, bison calves start eating grasses. Bison are herbivores.

Bison mothers stay close to their calves and protect them from predators such as wolves.

Calves become part of bison **herds**, or groups. Many herds have more than 50 bison.

Wolves from Canada

A long time ago, many wolves lived in the Yellowstone Ecosystem, but people killed them all. From 1995 to 1996, 31 wild gray wolves were brought to Yellowstone from Canada. Today, there are more than 100 wolves in Yellowstone.

elk

eagle

crow

beaver

brown
bear

coyote

gray
wolf

Helping other animals

In the past, the Yellowstone
wolves ate bison, but in Canada,
gray wolves hunted elk. Since
coming to Yellowstone, the wolves
from Canada have eaten many of
the elk in the park. By eating elk,
the wolves help other animals. Elk
eat young trees and other plants.
Fewer elk means more plants for
bears and beavers to eat. Wolves
often leave behind parts of the elk
they hunt. The elk leftovers are
food for crows, eagles, and coyotes.

23

Coyotes and wolves

This coyote is howling. Does it smell a wolf?

When the Canadian wolves came to Yellowstone, they killed many of the coyotes in the park. The coyotes that were left started howling more often to warn other coyotes that wolves were nearby. The coyote **packs**, or groups, then moved to new areas and started bigger packs. Bigger packs can better defend themselves against the wolves. People feel that coyotes and wolves will soon live together in a peaceful way in the Yellowstone Ecosystem.

After the wolves came, the coyote pups that were born were bigger, and there were more of them. More pups mean bigger coyote packs.

Coyotes and wolves look very much alike. Coyotes are smaller than wolves and have bigger ears. Which of the animals on this page is a coyote? Which is a gray wolf?

If this animal is a coyote, what is the animal in the picture above?

Yellowstone animal quiz

Match these clues to the pictures
of the animals on these two pages.
Which animal:
1. looks like a wolf?
2. is the biggest deer?
3. is called a raptor?
4. is a deer with huge ears?
5. is the biggest animal in Yellowstone?
6. belongs to the rabbit family?
7. is a cat?
8. is an omnivore?

bald eagle

*grizzly
bear*

bison

*mountain
lion*

pika

moose

mule deer

Answers:

1. A coyote looks like a wolf.
2. Moose are the biggest deer.
3. Bald eagles are raptors.
4. Mule deer have big ears.
5. Bison are the biggest animals.
6. Pikas are rabbit relatives.
7. Mountain lions are cats.
8. Grizzly bears are omnivores.

coyote

27

Supervolcano!

Much of Yellowstone National Park lies on top of a very old **volcano**. It is not just a volcano, it is a **supervolcano**! A volcano is an opening on the Earth's surface. Gases, ash, and hot, liquid rock called **magma**, can **erupt**, or burst out, of a volcano. Supervolcanoes are volcanoes that have had huge eruptions in the past. After a lot of magma pours out of a volcano, the center of the volcano falls inward, creating a **caldera**, or sunken area. The eruption of Yellowstone's supervolcano left a giant caldera. Much of Yellowstone is part of this super caldera.

Hot springs and geysers

Yellowstone is an **active** volcano. An active volcano is one that has erupted not long ago or one that may erupt in the future. There is a lot of magma not far below the Yellowstone caldera. The magma heats and powers the hot springs and geysers in Yellowstone. Hot springs are pools of water that are heated by volcanoes. Geysers are fountains that shoot boiling water and steam high into the sky.

Old Faithful is a geyser that erupts more often than any other big geyser—about every 91 minutes.

Grand Prismatic Spring is the largest hot spring in Yellowstone. The word "prismatic" describes something that shows the colors of the rainbow. The colors of this hot spring are red, orange, yellow, green, and blue.

29

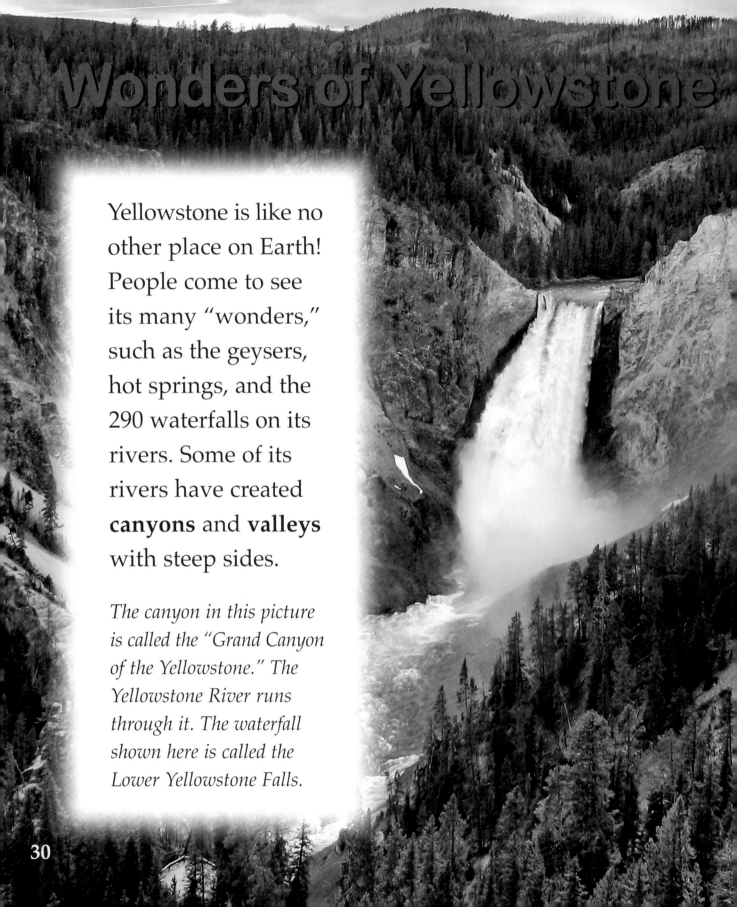

Yellowstone is like no other place on Earth! People come to see its many "wonders," such as the geysers, hot springs, and the 290 waterfalls on its rivers. Some of its rivers have created **canyons** and **valleys** with steep sides.

The canyon in this picture is called the "Grand Canyon of the Yellowstone." The Yellowstone River runs through it. The waterfall shown here is called the Lower Yellowstone Falls.

*At Mammoth Hot Springs, the springs have created **terraces**, or large steps, as well as some unusual shapes.*

Become a junior ranger!

There is a lot to see in Yellowstone—from volcanic "hot spots" to amazing animals. You can even become a Yellowstone Junior Ranger when you visit the park! The program will take you on a tour of the wonders of Yellowstone and teach you how you can help the animals in the park. To learn more about the ranger program, log on to: www.nps.gov/yell/forkids/beajuniorranger.htm

Glossary

Note: Some boldfaced words are defined where they appear in the book.

caldera A large hole that is created when a volcano collapses after a huge eruption

canyon A deep valley with steep sides

ecosystem Living and non-living things together in a certain area

energy The power living things get from food, which helps them move, grow, and stay healthy

food chain The pattern of eating and being eaten

geyser A fountain that shoots hot water high into the air

herd A large group of one kind of animal

hot spring A pool of water heated by a volcano

mating Joining together to make babies

national park A place where plants and animals are protected by a government

omnivore An animal that eats both plants and other animals

photosynthesis The process by which plants make food using sunlight, air, and water

raptor A bird that hunts other animals

valley Low land between mountains or hills, often with a river running through it

wetland An area of land that is under water some or all of the time

Index

Printed in the U.S.A.—BG